OUR CREATOR'S WORK

OUR CREATOR'S WORK

Thoughts of a Christian Poet

BILL PRICE

RESOURCE *Publications* • Eugene, Oregon

OUR CREATOR'S WORK
Thoughts of a Christian Poet

Resource Publications
An Imprint of Wipf and Stock Publishers
199 W. 8th Ave., Suite 3
Eugene, OR 97401

www.wipfandstock.com

PAPERBACK ISBN: 979-8-3852-5439-2
HARDCOVER ISBN: 979-8-3852-5440-8
EBOOK ISBN: 979-8-3852-5441-5

06/20/25

To my children and grandchildren with all my love

"All Scripture is breathed out by God and profitable for teaching, for reproof, for correction, and for training in righteousness, that the man of God may be complete, equipped for every good work."

(2 Timothy 3:16–17 KJV)

Contents

II. THOUGHTS OF NATURE
AND OUR WORLD

III. LIFE IS GIVEN TO US—
TO LEARN AND ENJOY

IV. LOVE
AND GROWING OLDER

V. DEATH
AND LIFE AFTER DEATH

V. I AM A SINNER
(AUTHOR'S CONCLUSION)

VII. APPENDIX

I

GOD AND THE CHRIST

WHY HE CAME

They said "Be quiet," when I chose Christ.
"If sharing—I shouldn't be bold.
I have no right to speak," they said;
"That story is not to be told."

My answer should never come as a surprise
For God Himself said, "Speak true."
And for that reason, I'll follow His steps
And do what he told us to do.

Jesus is like a doctor who comes
To help all the sick to heal.
There isn't a need for any physician
To help someone who's not ill.

Jesus came to heal the sick
And helped the blind to see.
He came to help all the sinners here,
Including you and me.

He even dined with prostitutes
And those hated by others.
He was inclusive—accepting all
The world's sisters and brothers.

He blessed all those who needed it
While offending those in charge
Who tried to showed how great they were
Compared to the people at large.

But most important, was what He did
By dying on Calvary's Cross.
He suffered and died for all mankind
To pay for the sins of the lost.

So, when they say, "You must not speak!"
I explain what rejection will cost.
Free will may allow them to choose what to do.
My choice is NOT to be lost.

"For God so loved the world, that he gave his only begotten Son, that whosoever believeth in him should not perish, but have everlasting life." (John 3:16 KJV)

SACRIFICE—ALL FOR WHAT?

There is no greater love on Earth than that of God above,
Who sent his Son to be a man and then, because of love,
Gave Him up as sacrifice to die for human sin,
So we could be forgiven and live with Him again.

And all for what? Why was this done?
A plan to show a victory won?
The plan of God, from High above?
The simple answer . . . GOD IS LOVE.

For all sin must be punished; there must be sacrifice,
To turn away the wrath of God. It's in His plan for life.
But now, instead of goats and sheep, to have our sins forgiven,
Jesus gave his life for us, so we could live in Heaven.

And all for what? Why was this done?
A plan to show a victory won?
The plan of God, from High above?
The simple answer . . . GOD IS LOVE.

Imagine you were standing there to watch our Savior's plight
Even God the Father turned; He couldn't bear the site.
While hanging on the cross for us, forgiving as He died,
With nails in hands and nails in feet, He was crucified.

And all for what? Why was this done?
A plan to show a victory won?
The plan of God, from High above?
The simple answer . . . GOD IS LOVE.

"Even when we were dead in sins, hath quickened us together with Christ, (by grace ye are saved;) And hath raised us up together, and made us sit together in heavenly places in Christ Jesus: That in the ages to come he might shew the exceeding riches of his grace in his kindness toward us through Christ Jesus." (Ephesians 2:4–6 KJV)

YES, I'M A SHEEP

I was told the other day
That I am but a sheep
Because I want to follow God,
But that's a choice I'll keep.

> And every time the Shepherd calls
> I'll listen to His voice
> Because of what He did for me.
> It's simply my own choice.

I did not use to feel this way.
I thought that I was free—
But now I know that I was blind
And God has let me see.

> You know that all must make a choice
> Because you are sheep too.
> So, you can follow world desires—
> Or choose a God that's true.

The Shepherd knows all of His sheep—
And He protects each one.
This Shepherd came and died for you
Because He is God's son.

"Verily, verily, I say unto you, He that entereth not by the door into the sheepfold, but climbeth up some other way, the same is a thief and a robber. But he that entereth in by the door is the shepherd of the sheep. To him the porter openeth; and the sheep hear his voice: and he calleth his own sheep by name, and leadeth them out. And when he putteth forth his own sheep, he goeth before them, and the sheep follow him: for they know his voice. And a stranger will they not follow, but will flee from him: for they know not the voice of strangers. This parable spake Jesus unto them: but they understood not what things they were which he spake unto them. Then said Jesus unto them again, Verily, verily, I say unto you, I am the door of the sheep." (John 10:7–10 KJV)

GOD IS REAL

I listened as he shouted out and stated "There's no God."
And if there's someone standing here—believing ... well—you're odd.
Prove to me that He exists—if you have a mind.
I've searched the whole world over and He's something I can't find."

I looked at him and quietly I said, "Excuse me sir,'
You don't believe, 'Cause you can't see. On that, I would concur.
But, let me ask you just one thing. is there love or hate?
Or, have you ever thought about a man that's ruled by fate?

You can't see love, you can't see hate, and then I know you can't
see fate.
But I can bet you surely feel that all of these are real.
So how about this thing called love? Is that something you see?
Or must you look to what the cause and the effect will be?"

Cause and effect will show you things that you would swear aren't
there.
You may not see the Lord above, but you can see His care.
When those who have just give to those who really are in need.
And do these thing unselfishly—there is a God, indeed.

When someone comforts one who's sad and wipes away their tears,
Or gives a hug to frightened folks to help to calm their fears,
When someone loves the 'least of these' and helps their heart to heal,
And does it just because of love, then that proves God is real."

"Verily I say unto you, Inasmuch as ye have done it unto one of the least of these my brethren, ye have done it unto me." (Matthew 25:40 KJV)

WHAT ARE THE ODDS?

There's a great story, and I'll tell you all this,
About a great Man that many dismiss
Because of the proof that people won't see.
They reject the truth and say this can't be.

The facts I present are from an old book—
The Old Testament—so just take a look—
This amazing fact presented by me
Concerns all the writing and old prophecies.

This very old book foretells that one man
Would someday be born to fulfill this plan,
Concerning salvation for all who agree
To accept Him completely while on bended knee.

What are the odds that one single man
Could fulfill all the words found in God's plan
Of a savior who came to set us all free
And lead us to Heaven for eternity.

Over 300 times, from the scriptures they wrote,
Beginning from Genesis where prophets spoke
Of a man, the Messiah, who would come to this earth
Who would be man and God from the time of His birth.

They spoke of His mother and of His birth place
They talked of his love, explaining His grace.
They said His descendants would surely be known
From the line of Judah and of King David's throne.

They told of the method in which He would die
Which was never used, and this is no lie,
During the time that they wrote of His death
They predicted the words upon His last breath.

They talked of this Man and His resurrection,
Of how He would teach, and of His connection
To Heaven and Earth, not thinking it odd,
The Messiah to come was surely from God.

What are the odds that the Jesus we know
Completed the prophecies of long ago?
The odds are more than we comprehend
Because Jesus was God, and that—I'll defend.

What would be the probability of one man fulfilling 353 messianic
prophecies? It must be astronomical. How could one man fulfill all these
prophecies? Professor Peter Stoner, distinguished professor of science
at Westmont College, with the help of six hundred students began by
calculating that the chance of one prophesy coming true, for example, a
man being born in Bethlehem (Micah 5:2), was one in 2.8 x 10 to the 5th
power—or rounded, one in 300,000. They took into consideration the
prophecy, measured all the components, and even took the probability of
men conspiring to fulfill a particular prophecy.[1]

1. Cady, "The Statistical Probability of Jesus Fulfilling the Messianic
Prophecies."

Next, they examined eight prophecies and, even after lowering the number to be very conservative, the answer was one in ten to the seventeenth power. In another calculation, Stoner examined forty-eight prophecies. He showed that probability of one man fulfilling forty-eight of them would be one in ten to the 157th power. That is a ten followed by 157 zeros. I wonder what the astronomical number associated with 324 would be. Stoner, himself, after his calculations, stated: "Any man who rejects Christ as the Son of God is rejecting a fact proved perhaps more absolutely than any other fact in the world." You do the math![2]

2. Schmidt, "Daily Devo: Fulfilled."

CREATION HAIKU

Science seems to claim
All things come with a big bang.
Accidents are we.

Churches tell us all
That God has created this
In his master plan.

If they're almost right—
Then God started the big bang
And that was his Plan.

If Science is wrong
Then this is how it began:
God created it

"In the beginning God created the heavens and the earth."
(Genesis 1:1 KJV)

GOD KNEW US BEFORE

I often question Natures words
Which tells of my creation
As if it were an accident
Which adds to my frustration.

The Universe, all by itself—
A giant "BANG" from nothing?
Well, I was taught that every action
must be caused by something.

And what about this human birth?
It, too, a chance event?
Or maybe God just planned it all
Before a baby's sent?

I looked to see if everything
Was under God's control—
Even that which we can't see
Which He has named a soul.

David gave a Psalm to us
Which has an explanation.
God knew us before our birth—
Before all His creation.

God knew us before we were
Created in the womb.
He also knows the day we must
Enter our own tomb.

We were given lives with souls,
From a God, with care,
And in The Book of Life, we'll find
Our names are written there.

"Then the word of the Lord came unto me, saying, before I formed thee in the belly I knew thee; and before thou camest forth out of the womb I sanctified thee, and I ordained thee a prophet unto the nations." (Jeremiah 1:4–5 KJV)

IS THERE?

There are those (I think them odd)
That swear to you there is no God.
They say that life is "nay" but grim
And they will not believe in Him.

I tell them with some peace of mind,
That if they look, they'll surely find
A little thing (I think a gem)
That truly God believes in them.

". . . But without faith it is impossible to please him: for he that cometh
to God must believe that he is, and that he is a rewarder of them that
diligently seek him." (Hebrews 11:6 KJV)

IF YOU WERE GIVEN

If you were given quite some time
To talk to anyone,
Even if the person picked,
Had already passed on.

Who would you choose, what personage,
To answer queries asked?
And, what's the most important one
That you would put to task?

The person I would choose to pick
Would have to know of faith,
And understand the reason that
My God has showed his grace.

And so, I know that I would pick
The one—and only one,
Who knew the father of us all,
Because He was His Son.

The questions I would choose to ask—
The ones I need to solve,
With someone I had chosen there,
Would probably involve
The definition of God's love
And why we seem to find

That this one simple attribute
Is hard for humankind.

"Let the morning bring me word of your unfailing love, for I have put my trust in you. Show me the way I should go, for to you I entrust my life." (Psalm 143:8 KJV)

CAN I GET A WITNESS?

It is our duty, as a child of God,
To hear His word and then to make a choice.
Our purpose is to follow Jesus Christ
And then explain the Gospel in one Voice.

Two witnesses will come to show the World
That soon The Lord's return will surely be
What John had seen and told in Revelation
(Those Witnesses described as Olive Trees).

Some people say that these two witnesses
Are Moses and Elijah filled with power.
Others swear it's Enoch and Elijah
Preaching here in Mankind's final hours.

Another thought is that there's someone else
Who the apostle John was speaking of,
It is "completed" Jews and Christians, too
Who will receive their power from up above.

The Word of God explains the Olive Tree
And also speaks of "gentile" Olive shoots.
The two, though different, both accepted Christ.
They also say that both grow from His roots.

We know the time when Peter walked the Earth,
And John, with him, used power from above
To heal the sick, performing miracles,
That showed mankind the power of God's love.

When these two witness receive their power
They, too, will show the miracles of Christ,
Explaining that it's time for Man's repentance
So new believers find eternal life.

These two will have the power of life and death.
Preach three- and one-half years for all it's worth.
The two will be defeated by the Beast,
To bring about the reign on of Christ on Earth.

The point is not to argue which is right,
The point is that all followers endeavor
To live a life that shows the love of Christ
And gladly serve our Savior here forever.

"And I will give power unto my two witnesses, and they shall prophesy
a thousand two hundred and threescore days, clothed in sackcloth"
(Revelation 11:3–4 KJV)

BEHOLD THE LAMB

They ask me why I celebrate
As Christmas time draws near.
I answered very simply that
I love this time of year.

I tell them of a baby born
in such a lowly place—
(that manger in a stable stall)
To save the human race.

They said, "It's not a kingly place,
So cold and so forlorn."
I look at them and merely ask,
Where would a lamb be born?

"The next day John sees Jesus coming unto him, and saith, Behold the Lamb of God, which takes away the sin of the world." (John 1:29 KJV)

THE SACRIFICIAL BLOOD

The morning mist evaporates
In the rising sun.
The dew drops do not hesitate
To leave earth one by one.

It is the presence of the sun,
Which makes it crystal clear,
No fog or haze will linger on
When warming rays appear.

Like the sun that takes away
The darkness and the night,
So, too, the Son will keep at bay
All sins that souls must fight.

The reason that He came to Earth
was purely done for love—
A spotless soul—so pure at birth,
Who came down from above.

In the days before the Christ, whenever man would sin,
The Law required sacrifice for forgiveness to begin.
So, God came down in human form fulfilling all the Law.
He took our sin upon Himself and shed His blood for all.

"How much more shall the blood of Christ, who through the eternal Spirit offered himself without spot to God, purge your conscience from dead works to serve the living God?" (Hebrews 9:14 KJV)

ISAIAH SAID IT FIRST

(Years before The Christ was born)

Who was He that grew like tender shoots
From the ground and from majestic root?
Did He appear as some seductive fire?
Was he created for our own desire?

No!—He was The One rejected by mankind.
His body suffered and His words maligned,
Like someone other people would reject
And look at with the lowest of respect.

Oh, but in truth, He took our every pain
And bore our suffering—and all our strain.
Yet, we perceived it punishment from God
Just like a dad who never spared the rod.

It was for our transgressions—His blood ran.
He died and took the sins of every man.
He brought us peace, and took our punishment,
And by His wounds our very souls were cleansed.

This Shepard calls us sheep who've gone astray.
As human kind—we always want our way.
And it was God who said this Man could fall
And take away the sinfulness of all.

They beat Him 'till His body was blood stained.
He never spoke a word through all the pain.
He faced His false accusers with no voice,
Like lambs led to slaughter without choice.

Isaiah spoke these words of prophesy
About a sinless man and who He'd be:
The Son of God who came and chose to die,
So, we could live forever by His side.

"But he was wounded for our transgressions, he was bruised for our iniquities: the chastisement of our peace was upon him; and with his stripes we are healed." (Isaiah 53:5 KJV)

WHAT GOD YOU SERVE: A SONNET

What God you serve is really up to you.
I've made my choice and—this advice I give:
The choice you make is your decision, too
And once decided that is how you'll live

For me, I love the God of Abraham,
The One who sent his son to die for me.
You understand that that's the way I am.
For that is how I was brought up to be.

Some people say that they will serve no God;
The very thought—they just cannot conceive.
Although I think them to be very odd,
I will accept their right to not believe.

From my beliefs I know I will not budge,
But this I promise you—I will not Judge.

"And if it seem evil unto you to serve the LORD, choose you this day
whom ye will serve; whether the gods which your fathers served that
were on the other side of the flood, or the gods of the Amorites, in whose
land ye dwell: but as for me and my house, we will serve the LORD."
(Joshua 24:15 KJV)

FEARING GOD

When I was young, I was afraid of dark things in the night.
Strange noises pounced upon my ears and logic took its flight.
I grew to understand dark things not always in my sight,
Became some object to respect—then, logic ruled the night.

Fear of God is much the same
For all who won't believe.
It's separation from a God
Who they just can't conceive.

It is a fear of Judgment Day with everlasting strife—
A fear of facing punishment, without eternal life.
For all of those who accept God there is a difference.
It is based upon respect—with awe and reverence.

It's wise discernment—true wisdom
Of a God who will always be—
The great Creator of us all—
Giving life eternally.

"As free, and not using your liberty for a cloke of maliciousness, but as
the servants of God. Honour all men. Love the brotherhood. Fear God.
Honour the king" (1Peter 2: 16–17 KJV)

HIS SEVEN I AM'S

"I am the light of the world" Christ said,
And the Pharisees challenged him.
They asked Him who He thought He was.
His answer to them was, "I Am."

Jesus also used the words
"I Am the Bread of Life."
Explaining He ends the hunger we have
And eliminates all of our strife.

"I AM the Door of the Sheep." He said.
The only one you will see—
That lets the sheep be safe from harm.
And "No one comes in, but by me."

"I AM the Good Shepherd" He said in John.
A promise He'd surely keep.
As any Shepard would do for his flock;
He'd give His life for His sheep.

"I AM the Resurrection," He cried,
Followed by, "and the Life."
He was explaining that He was the source
To continue to live when we die.

"I AM the Way, the Truth and the Life."
He said He was more than God's son.
"You've seen your Father if you have seen me,
For I and the Father are one."

When Jesus expressed, "I AM the True Vine."
And disciples would all bear good fruit,
He explained how all the branches would live
Because He was their nurturing root.

Jesus declared "I AM" seven times,
Like the God of Abraham
Said to Moses, who asked Him for His name
And He answered, "I Am That I Am."

"Your father Abraham rejoiced to see my day: and he saw it, and was glad. Then said the Jews unto him, Thou art not yet fifty years old, and hast thou seen Abraham. Jesus said unto them, Verily, verily, I say unto you, Before Abraham was, I am." (John 8: 56–58 KJV)

THEY BOTH ARE "I AM"

"I AM that I AM said God through the fire
I know all your needs and all you desire.
He loved you so much that He sent His own Son
To take on our sins and to suffer each one.

Our Jesus was ready—a sacrificed Lamb.
They asked, are you God? And he answered "I AM."
We no longer fear—for we all will see Heaven
When we accept Him—this one God has given.

So, who was His Son—this Jesus, by name?
It happens to be that they're one and the same.
For God is the Father and God is the Son.
With the Holy Spirit—That makes three in one!

"Therefore the Jews sought the more to kill him, because he not only
had broken the sabbath, but said also that God was his Father, making
himself equal with God." (John 5:18 KJV)

II

THOUGHTS OF NATURE
AND OUR WORLD

ALL THINGS ARE "THREE"

I'm often asked why I believe,
As many Christians do,
How I could think the Trinity
Could possibly be true.

I'll look at them and form a smile
And then I will reply.
This concept isn't hard to see
And here's your answers why.

Look out at all our Universe
See all the things in space?
Everything we see is "three"[1]
A concept I embrace.

Looking at our Universe,
We see what we expect—
It's height and width and length combined
Are "Three" things we detect.

How about a closer look,
With humans living there
The "three" things that sustain our life
Is water, earth, and air.[2]

1. The universe is thought to consist of three types of substance: normal matter, "dark matter" and "dark energy." See NASA.gov, "Building Blocks."
2. The biosphere is made of three parts, called the lithosphere, atmosphere

The Earth itself has "three" main parts:
The Mantle, Crust, and Core.
The types of rocks are also "three"[3]
As further we explore.

And how about our water here?[4]
Which we must have—or die.
The facts won't change—we find a "three"
No matter how we try.

In the Universe of "Threes."
Living things contain,
Dividing by genetic rules,
That which we call "Domain"[5]

From childhood—puberty—old age
We contain some "threes"
Our makeup is from DNA
(A, T, C, or G).[6]

and hydrosphere. See Mac, "What Are The 3 Parts Of The Biosphere?"

3. The Earth is composed of three separate layers. These are the crust, the mantle and the core, and the three types of rocks are: igneous, metamorphic, and sedimentary. See Panchuk, "Earth's Layers."

4 Water is made of two hydrogen and one oxygen atoms. The three main parts of the water cycle would be Evaporation, Condensation, and then Precipitation. Three forms of water are solid, liquid, gas. It is odorless, colorless., and tasteless. See Examples.com, "Water (H20)."

5. Living things on Earth are divided into three groups based on genetic similarities which is called Domain. See EarthHow "What are the 3 Domains of Life?"

6. Human life contains childhood, puberty, old age, but our DNA consists of three parts, too: sugar, phosphate, and a nitrogen base (A, T, C, or G) aka, the three-part unit. See NIH, "Deoxyribonucleic Acid (DNA) Fact Sheet."

Long ago our science said
Small Atoms divide by three.[7]
Then they found the "three" part Quark—
The smallest we could see.

So, ask again why I believe
That God contains a "three"
I think there is no question now.
God has made it be.[8] (10)

"The grace of the Lord Jesus Christ, and the love of God, and the communion of the Holy Ghost, be with you all." (2 Corinthians 13:14 KJV)

7. Life is made up of atoms: protons, electrons, and neutrons, but the smallest particle known to man, at this point, is the quark. There are three quarks that make up a neutron. See Microsoft Bing, "Three Parts of the Atom and Quarks."

8. Man is made in the image of God. God is three in one and man is made of three: body spirit, and soul. See Bible.org, "Man Is Made in the Image of God."

GOD HAS MADE THE RAINBOW

A rainbow fills the sky—

                green
        blue   yellow
    indigo   orange
    violet   red

And The Promise Continues.

[After the flood]

"I do set my bow in the cloud, and it shall be for a token of a covenant between me and the earth." (Genesis 9:13 KJV)

LILY FIELD

I came upon a lily field,
While on a path both old and worn.
The barren dirt beneath my feet
Showed the travelers it had borne.

I stood upon the flattened earth
And felt the dead and beaten grass
And gazed toward the lily field—
An obvious contrast.

I stood awhile and looked at both,
My thoughts raced 'tween the new and old.
I thought of death; I thought of life
In fields of purple, white, and gold.

I've often seen life's hurt and pain,
But at that time my heart was healed.
My eyes beheld the meaning there
While looking at the lily field.

"And why take ye thought for raiment? Consider the lilies of the field,
how they grow; they toil not, neither do they spin: And yet I say unto
you, That even Solomon in all his glory was not arrayed like one of these.
(Matthew 6:28–29 KJV)

CARNATIONS

I never thought a flower
Could mean so many things.
But now I know the colors found
Each, a different message brings.

I looked at the carnations.
It showed impressive power.
The name, itself, comes from the Greeks
And means a "Heavenly Flower.

It comes in red and white
And pink, and purple hue;
Each one a diverse message
For all the world to view.

Light red carnations represent
Someone's admiration.
Dark red flowers indicate
A love and some affection

White carnations represent
Deep love and luck to change.
But one that's white and also striped
Shows love that's not exchanged.

Purple flowers indicate
Someone's capriciousness.
Or it becomes a funeral flower
To show condolences.

According to an early tale,
The first pink one appeared
The hour Jesus bore His cross.
It sprung from Mary's tears.

This carnation's messages—With all its colors and powers
Represents the "New Year" month—It's January's flower.

"For behold, the winter is past; the rain is over and gone. The flowers
appear on the earth, the time of singing has come . . ."
(Song of Solomon 2:11–12 KJV)

THE ARTIST

A canvas is a waste of space.
It doesn't mean so much,
Unless the artist fills it with
A grand artistic touch.

Whatever picture that appears
Comes from the artist's heart.
The careful lines are what make it
Become a piece of art.

It's through the talent of the one
Who goes through pain and strife,
To take the empty canvases and
Bring them all to life.

"But now, O LORD, thou art our father; we are the clay, and thou our
potter; and we all are the work of thy hand. (Isaiah 64:8 KJV)

THE OLD FARMER'S BARN

I saw it still standing beside the oak tree.
The redness had faded, but I could still see
That the memories formed there were all in my mind
And nothing erased it—not even time.

I walked even closer and opened the door
And went on inside and sat on the floor.
Feeling cracked wood beneath my cracked hand,
I remembered I grew up as part of this land.

I saw visions of fishing within my mind's eye
And focused on knots that I tied to make flies.

I could still see the water that just lay beyond
The big willow tree that grew near the pond.

I remembered the hot sun and how it would beat
Down on the horses while tails fanned the heat.
I could still see the cattle who walked one by one
Through the gate of the barnyard, when the milking was done.

I would never forget how I grew up out here;
How I worked every day throughout the whole year.
How I fed all the creatures from spring to the fall
And helped, in the winter, when they stayed in their stall.

I may have grown old and my steps may have slowed,
But I'll never forget what a wonder life showed.
I'll never regret all my days on the farm,
As I sit with my memories in my little red barn.

"Be patient therefore, brethren, unto the coming of the Lord. Behold, the husbandman waiteth for the precious fruit of the earth, and hath long patience for it, until he receive the early and latter rain." (James 5:7 KJV)

THE LIGHT THROUGH US

God created light to pierce the dark,
And others see His light within our heart;
So, we will try to live out every day
To show our neighbors we observe God's way.

We may become distracted and distressed
But God will always help—when we need rest.
Persecution may affect our life.
But Christ will not forsake us in our strife.

They'll cast us down—we'll feel demoralized.
But what God says, what He has authorized,
Can never take away our faith and love
That shows the light, through us, of Christ above.

"Let your light so shine before men, that they may see your good works, and glorify your Father which is in heaven." (Matthew 5:16 KJV)

MOUNTAIN'S MAJESTY

My early journey took me to
The peaks of Majesty.
I traveled to restore my soul
And see what I could see.

I started looking toward the east
To watch a new sunrise.
The colors, woken by the sun,
Were pleasant to my eyes.

And when I looked toward south and north,
I saw a wondrous sight.
The darkness there had disappeared.
And nature danced with light.

I stayed all day and watch the world
I was the mountain's guest,
And then I watched the sun go down
As I was facing west.

I was walking home that night—Through grass and rock and sod,
I knew my trip had been worthwhile,—And I felt close to God.

"How beautiful upon the mountains are the feet of him that bringeth good
tidings, that publisheth peace; that bringeth good tidings of good, that pub-
lisheth salvation; that saith unto Zion, Thy God reigneth." (Isaiah 52:7 KJV)

ODE TO A CLOUD

To you, oh cloud, who silently
Drifts upon the wind,
I oft' have wondered what you've seen
And places you have been.

You, floating by and looking down
On human strife and strain,
Is it you who cries for them
And shows them tears of rain?

Is it with your sisters there,
Who share the skies with you,
That makes you smile upon the world
And let the sun shine through?

I lay upon the fresh cut field
And watch you change and part.
Is it imagination that
Has turned you into Art?

Or are you simply showing us
What you have seen from birth?
Are you creating pictures there
That you observed on earth?

To you, oh cloud, who silently
Drifts upon the wind,
I oft' have wondered what you've seen
And places you have been.

"Dost thou know the balancings of the clouds, the wondrous works of
him which is perfect in knowledge?" (Job 37:16 KJV)

TO THE MOON

The softness of reflected light—

God's creation in the night—

That causes women soon to swoon—

Oh, Shine on bright and faithful moon.

Cast your beams, let your light yield,

As lovers lie in golden fields—

A soft and gentle shining care—

A glow upon your lovers there.

"It shall be established for ever as the moon, and as a faithful witness in heaven. Selah." (Psalm 89:37 KJV)

MEMORIES OF THE KNOTTY PINE

The wood, cut from the knotty pine,
Was used to make these walls.
The memories came back to me
As I walked down these halls.

The scents that still filled up the air—
The smell of firewood—
Reminded me of the winters there
And times when life was good.

I would watch the fire's glow
Within the fireplace.
The shadows almost seemed to grow
Across the piney space.

My heart was filled, remembering
The walls of knotty pine.
Each and every memory
Always will be mine.

"Peace be within thy walls, and prosperity within thy palaces!"
(Psalm 122:7 KJV)

TO THE EAGLE

Sailing on the updraft wind
Among the clouds on high,
With spread of wing and talons sharp
Majestic eagle fly.

With arrows clutched to signify
The hero's willing take
To live, to fight, or maybe die,
And all for freedom's sake.

And in the other grasping tight
A sprig of olive leaf,
To show the willingness, through might,
To offer lasting peace.

Oh, eagle soar upon your height
With eyes on land below,
And through your strength and through your flight
To all—your glory show.

"But they that wait upon the Lord shall renew their strength; they shall
mount up with wings as eagles; they shall run, and not be weary; and
they shall walk, and not faint." (Isaiah 40:31 KJV)

BUTTERFLY

I sat upon my little chair watching the garden grow.
I was a child with little thoughts that I just had to know.

What made the flowers, in their beds, sprout and bloom in full?
What made the plants, in morning light, appear to be a jewel?

And then, while sitting quietly, I saw a butterfly
It didn't quench my need to know, or seek to answer why?

The butterfly, on gentle wings, flits with little power.
And sometimes, as I watch it flit, it moved from flower to flower.

Had someone there, if there someone, taught her what to do?
Or how to spread the pollen there, as butterflies will do?

I never found, while looking on a solid answer why,
This flying thing, in love with flowers, was called the butterfly.

When I grew up, and science taught me many reasons why,
I still must question, with a sigh,—who has taught the butterfly?

"Therefore if any man be in Christ, he is a new creature: old things are passed away; behold, all things are become new." (2 Cor. 5:17 KJV)

THE WATERFALL

My mind is tamed, my soul complete.
My face is cooled, the air is sweet.
I rest my tired aching feet,
While eyes provide me nature's treat.

I sit below the gentle falls
And meditate with nature calls.
Surrounding me are rocky walls
That produce the waterfalls.

The scene always remained the same
Every time I went and came.
And every time, it's just a shame,
I wish that I could still remain.

But, when I leave the beauty there,
My mind becomes so crystal clear.
To view creation, that's so dear,
I know that God has put it here.

"Deep calleth unto deep at the noise of thy waterspouts: all thy waves and
thy billows are gone over me." (Psalm 42:7 KJV)

"For ye shall go out with joy, and be led forth with peace: the mountains
and the hills shall break forth before you into singing, and all the trees of
the field shall clap their hands." (Isaiah 55:12 KJV)

COMPLETING WINTER DAYS

Snowflakes fall, then gently float
And kiss the mountain's face,
Creating nature's winter scene
Like shawls of dainty lace.

And on the hillside piling high,
The snows create a mound.
Childlike laughs replete the air
As sleds go up and down.

Nothing satisfies the heart
More than naive play.
Joyful sounds echo the land
Completing winter days.

While the earth remaineth, seedtime and harvest, and cold and heat, and
summer and winter, and day and night shall not cease."
(Genesis 8:22 KJV)

SPRING'S BIRTH

Winter, with its gasp of last cold breath,
    Brings song and cooing of the Turtledove—

Which wakens Spring, who's colors fill the land.
    And all the world's alive with thoughts of love.

Solomon, with all his passions put to song—
    And all the thoughts the words of Shakespeare bring.
Pale in comparison to mother Earth
    They are not equal to birth pangs of spring.

It is the time when all things become new,
    While sounds of Nature's melody give Birth,
Painting life—with all the palette hues
    And fragrant joys envelop all the Earth.

"For everything there is a season, and a time for every matter under heaven." (Ecclesiastes 3:1 KJV)

OUT OF NOTHING

Every tiny speck
In the universe
Is of such importance
I must put it to verse.

The reason it's so precious
The reason this means something
God said "be"—and it existed—
Created out of nothing.

Before there was a time—
Before space was conceived—
Simple words created all—
God stated "let it be."

"Through faith we understand that the worlds were framed by the word of God, so that things which are seen were not made of things which do appear." (Hebrews 11:3 KJV)

III

LIFE IS GIVEN TO US—
To Learn And Enjoy

Life

CONSIDER LIFE

Consider life with all its joys,
Its pain, and sadness too.
Consider all that causes this
No matter what you do.

Some would say that every day
Is planned out just for you.
Others say your fate's your own
As you see your life through.

I believe you make your life
(an empty slate to fill)
What you want it to become
Because you have free will.

So if you should let go of good
And evil takes control,
Then your lives will empty be.
The pain will take its toll.

If you believe that you'll succeed
And look for good results,
Then you'll be fine—you'll do just great.
You'll work to clear your faults.

For everyone must choose a path
And do what he must do;
Whether it be fate or choice,
Your life is up to you.

"For, brethren, ye have been called unto liberty; only use not liberty for an occasion to the flesh, but by love serve one another."
(Galatians 5:13 KJV)

I BELIEVE

I believe in this
And you believe in that.
You are right and I am wrong,
And that is where we're at!
    I believe in that
    And you believe in this.
    You are wrong and I am right,
    But something is amiss.
Yes, we disagree—
But we need not be shallow.
Why insist we hurt each other
With our slings and arrows?
    The concepts you embrace—
    The thoughts that I have brought,
    Most likely are created by
    The way that we were taught.
Any different viewpoint
Should not be fraught with hate.
Bickering and fighting
Cannot rule our debate.
    Shouldn't you and I
    Agree to disagree,
    But as we bring up different thought,
    Do it agreeably?

"A wrathful man stirreth up strife: but he that is slow to anger appeaseth
strife." (Proverbs 15:18 KJV)

NEW WORLD

I came into this brand-new world
Through a tunnel filled with light.
I didn't know what to expect,
But knew that it was right.

Within that light, I saw shadows
I didn't understand.
I then looked at a loving face
That held me in his hand.

I recognized some voices there
That I had heard before.
I somehow knew the people here;
And soon I saw some more.

They kept on coming to greet me there,
and some showed me around.
I never knew it would be like this—
This joy that I had found.

Oh yes, my travel to this world
was filled with every fright.
I think that I had been elsewhere,
When I came through the light.

I'm glad that I could travel to
This land with love so pure.
It caused me almost to forget
Where I had been before.

But as I thought of how I'd come
to be a part of this.
I remembered those I'd left-
So many I would miss.

I knew I had to leave them there,
I hoped they'd understand
They, too, will have to face the light
And travel to this land.

Oh, now that I could see so clear
I thought that this new birth,
Was so much better than I had,
When I had lived on Earth.

"And he shewed me a pure river of water of life, clear as crystal, proceeding out of the throne of God and of the Lamb. In the midst of the street of it, and on either side of the river, was there the tree of life, which bare twelve manner of fruits, and yielded her fruit every month: and the leaves of the tree were for the healing of the nations. And there shall be no more curse: but the throne of God and of the Lamb shall be in it; and his servants shall serve him: And they shall see his face; and his name shall be in their foreheads. And there shall be no night there; and they need no candle, neither light of the sun; for the Lord God giveth them light: and they shall reign for ever and ever." (Revelation 22: 1–5 KJV)

SMILES

I walk around most of my days
With smiles upon my face.
I'd rather live a life that's fun,
With happiness and grace.

To live each day depressed and sad
To me—is a mistake.
I want to live a life that's full.
I'll do what e'er it takes.

To help another form a smile,
One must give one away.
And soon you'll see the consequence—
A thousand smiles a day.

"A merry heart maketh a cheerful countenance: but by sorrow of the heart the spirit is broken." (Proverbs 15:13 KJV)

UNKNOWN AND UNWANTED

She sat beside the shopping cart
And waded through her wares.
She sorted this and reached for that
And settled for a tattered hat.

She reached toward a garbage bin
And searched the contents found within.
She grabbed a wrinkled bag of meat
To find a bit of food to eat.

No one saw her sitting there
Until a man of means
Stopped to give his lunch to her
And sat with her, unseen.

He took some time and said a prayer
And asked for God to bless
This lady who had naught to do,
But sit among her mess.

He didn't have to stop each day
To take the time and share.
He did it all out of love;
To show that someone cared.

He never helped for some reward,
Or for some others praise.
He didn't give for earthly gain
Or any accolades.

He gave to her and sat with her
To show a kind of love,
That he believed all man should do
As taught by God above.

Therefore all things whatsoever ye would that men should do to you, do ye even so to them: for this is the law and the prophets." (Matthew 7:12 KJV)

BACK THEN

Playing in the street, with friends around the block.
There was no want for proper gear, or need to watch a clock.

Hours passing by, parked cars became a base,
A well-worn ball and sticks for bats, and life—a slower pace.

The clothes we wore weren't new, our jeans a little worn,
Every day we played in them. that's why the knees were torn.

We played the whole day through, until the sun was gone.
We knew we had to go straight home, when street lights would
    turn on.

We didn't have much cash; we didn't really care.
We never owned expensive things, but we were happy there.

While reminiscing here, and writing of "back then,"
We miss our streets and neighborhood, 'Cause life was simple then.

"Not that I speak in respect of want: for I have learned, in whatsoever
state I am, therewith to be content. I know both how to be abased,
and I know how to abound: everywhere and in all things I am

instructed both to be full and to be hungry, both to abound and to suffer need. I can do all things through Christ which strengtheneth me." (Philippians 4:11–13 KJV)

MOTHER

I thought back to the life I chose,
As day and day passed by,
And realized all the things I know
I learned at Mother's side.

The way I look at others,
And the way I see the Earth,
I learned by watching Mother
As she taught about our worth.

I watched her as she treated folks
With love and not disdain,
And all the pains and worldly yokes
She bore with no complaints.

When I did wrong and made mistakes,
I did not fear the rod.
I learned that Mother taught me well,
By listening to God.

"Train up a child in the way he should go: and when he is old, he will not depart from it." (Proverbs 22:6 KJV)

WHAT WOULD YOU LOSE?

In this modern world that won't deal with fact,
And feelings control each human act,
Then conflicts rise using anti-God speak.
And Christians are those who are taking the heat.

> But it's nothing new in a world that's odd.
> People have always turned from God.
> Jesus is someone they won't believe in.
> They'd rather choose a life full of sin.

People ask Christians, "Just what is the cost
If we have some fun in a world that is lost?
There's nothing to come after we're dead,
So why not enjoy this world instead?"

> But as a man who believes in the Lord.
> I tell them that I can little afford
> To live a life that is centered on me
> And lose the life of eternity.

If I live for God and find that you're right,
And there is just darkness instead of the light,
Then why not be kind and love every day,
And what have I lost in living this way?

But if I am right and they should still choose
To live selfishly—then what do they lose?
A life after death—a life up above.
An eternity that will be filled with God's love.

"So, then they that are in the flesh cannot please God. But ye are not in
the flesh, but in the Spirit, if so be that the Spirit of God dwell in you.
Now if any man have not the Spirit of Christ, he is none of his. And if
Christ be in you, the body is dead because of sin; but the Spirit is life
because of righteousness." (Romans 8:8–10 KJV)

I WAS RAISED UP

I was raised up by my dad to understand the need
To live a life full of hard work and good and honest deeds.

And I was raised up by mother dear to give up earthly greed.
The willingness to help others was all I'd really need.

When hard work brings some "pleasure" things, then happiness is
   there.
But only if, as I have found, one helps and gives and shares.

I think it wise to follow what my dad and mom have taught.
Love and caring is what one needs to live the way we ought.

"I have shewed you all things, how that so laboring ye ought to support
the weak, and to remember the words of the Lord Jesus, how he said, It is
more blessed to give than to receive." (Acts 20: 35 KJV)

CASTLES

Castles built upon the sand
Will never last all day.
Ebbs and flows of waters there
Will wash the sand away.

Castles built upon the rocks
Will never wash away.
Firm foundations chosen are
For castles built to stay.

Life is like a castle built
Upon a rock or sand.
The foundations that you choose
Will make it fall or stand.

"Therefore whosoever heareth these sayings of mine, and doeth them, I will liken him unto a wise man, which built his house upon a rock: And the rain descended, and the floods came, and the winds blew, and beat upon that house; and it fell not: for it was founded upon a rock and every one that heareth these sayings of mine, and doeth them not, shall be likened unto a foolish man, which built his house upon the sand: And the rain descended, and the floods came, and the winds blew, and beat upon that house; and it fell: and great was the fall of it." (Matthew 7: 24–27 KJV)

SINCE TIME BEGAN

Oh why, Oh why, since time began,
Has man felt the need to kill fellow man?
Why has there been a need within them
To end other lives whenever they can.

Will there ever, ever be
A time where man begins to see
He must not live by sword and knife
While finding it easy to take a life.

When will there be a time for man
To help someone whenever he can.
When will he learn for him to give—
Is better than killing. Let others live!

It is about time for man to think
And begin to see a positive link
Between a happiness that could be found
And a peace he creates the world around.

Oh, STOP causing rivers to turn blood red.
It's your warring and fighting that causes these dead.
Oh, stop all this madness and grief and the strife;
Please find a way to bring love to this life.

From this very moment throw down your weapon.
Just share what you have. Do what you can
To teach that this killing and dying should cease,
So that, finally, man will find lasting peace.

"Thou shalt not murder." (Exodus 20:13 KJV)

"Then said Jesus unto him, Put up again thy sword into his place: for all
they that take the sword shall perish with the sword." (Matthew 26:52 KJV)

SOW AND REAP

Plant your seed and watch it sprout.
Water it each day.
What will happen? There's no doubt.
Your plant is here to stay.

Live your life and water it
While giving with a smile.
Loving others as yourself,
Will make your life worthwhile.

And all your happiness will show—
And all that love will keep
You realizing—what you sow
Is what you'll also reap.

"Be not deceived; God is not mocked: for whatsoever a man soweth, that shall he also reap. For he that soweth to his flesh shall of the flesh reap corruption; but he that soweth to the Spirit shall of the Spirit reap life everlasting." (Galatians 6:7–8 KJV)

"DON'T LET THE SUN
GO DOWN UPON YOUR WRATH."

(Ephesians 4:26)

Don't close your eyes, don't try to rest,
Don't fall to sleep, pretend you're blessed—
You're the one who'll end up sad,
Because inside you are still mad.

Don't let the sun fall in the west
If you have anger—not addressed.
You'll lay awake and wish you had
Done what's right to make you glad.

Follow lessons from above
And turn that anger back to love.
Don't let the sun go down—in wrath
You should take the higher path.

Resolve that which has caused you pain,
So, you can calmly rest your brain.
Reconcile so love will reign.
Peace in your soul is what you'll gain.

"Be ye angry, and sin not: let not the sun go down upon your wrath"
(Ephesians 4:26 KJV)

"Let all bitterness, and wrath, and anger, and clamor, and evil speaking, be put away from you, with all malice: And be ye kind one to another, tenderhearted, forgiving one another, even as God for Christ's sake hath forgiven you." (Ephesians 4:31–32 KJV)

YESTERDAY, TODAY, AND TOMORROW

Yesterday, I was too young
To know that life was a fleeting thing.
I had all the world at my fingertips—
A kingdom where I was the king.

To me, my time was infinite,
With not a care in the world,
Like a ship with full and billowy sails,
My life before me—unfurled.

Today I think I'm at that age where life
Passes by with speed.
Many things aren't in my reach
Like a knight without his steed.

To me my time is never enough
I approach at a cautious pace,
Like a boat with torn and ragged sails,
My life has slowed its race.

Tomorrow I'll reached that age in life
That accepts what time can give.
My world will be filled with memories
Of a life that was fully lived.

To me my time will be well spent
Sharing all the things I have seen,
Like the ship that provided quite a few tales
Recounting the places it's been.

" Lo, children are an heritage of the Lord: and the fruit of the womb is his reward. As arrows are in the hand of a mighty man; so are children of the youth." (Psalm 127:3–4 KJV)

"The glory of young men is their strength: and the beauty of old men is the grey head." (Proverbs 20:29 KJV)

"The Gray head is a crown of glory, if it be found in the way of righteousness." (Proverbs 16:31 KJV)

FULL ARMOR

Why must we wear the full armor of God
Protecting ourselves from our head to our feet?
What is the battle that we're training for?
Who are the ones we'll defeat?

> Our battle is not with the flesh and the blood;
> We fight against leaders of darkness.
> We train to fight those who possess evil powers
> And those full of dark wickedness.

We put on our helmets, our breastplates, our shields
And we fight for our Lord God above.
We show them the truth and the righteousness
And we do it with peace and with love.

> So why must we wear the full armor of God
> And continue to pray constantly?
> We fight the good fight to spread our god's word,
> Share the gospel, and its mysteries.

"Finally, my brethren, be strong in the Lord, and in the power of his
might. Put on the whole armour of God, that ye may be able to stand
against the wiles of the devil. For we wrestle not against flesh and
blood, but against principalities, against powers, against the rulers of
the darkness of this world, against spiritual wickedness in high places.
Wherefore take unto you the whole armour of God, that ye may be

able to withstand in the evil day, and having done all, to stand. Stand therefore, having your loins girt about with truth, and having on the breastplate of righteousness; And your feet shod with the preparation of the gospel of peace; Above all, taking the shield of faith, wherewith ye shall be able to quench all the fiery darts of the wicked. And take the helmet of salvation, and the sword of the Spirit, which is the word of God: Praying always with all prayer and supplication in the Spirit, and watching thereunto with all perseverance and supplication for all saints; And for me, that utterance may be given unto me, that I may open my mouth boldly, to make known the mystery of the gospel, For which I am an ambassador in bonds: that therein I may speak boldly, as I ought to speak." (Ephesians 6:10–20 KJV)

SONNET FOR A LIFE LIKE JOB

I never thought that life could turn so hard,
Or memories could cause hearts to be scarred.
I can't believe it only takes one day
For life to change in such a harmful way.

Well just consider what life did to Job.
(A story one has heard around the globe.)
This man of God, who Satan did assail
And caused the things within his life to fail.

He lost his wealth and health and then his wife,
And everything was taken from his life.
Then God returned him to a life of bliss
Because he would not blame his God for this.

So even if we live life painfully
This story teaches us to faithful be.

"Behold, we count them happy which endure. Ye have heard of the
patience of Job, and have seen the end of the Lord; that the Lord is very
pitiful, and of tender mercy." (James 5:11 KJV)

WALLS

There is an argument today—
Dividing folks in every way,
And causing some with wicked zeal
To shout about the way they feel.

The argument of which I speak
Concerns a wall of which some seek—
A wall, they say will guarantee America's security.
Others say that such a wall

Shows the country's sad downfall.
Walls are an immoral sign
designed by those who are unkind.
I look at those who shout out loud

To convince an unsure crowd
That we don't need a border zone—
Yet, they're protected by their own.

Whenever people disagree,
I ask that some would hear my plea.
I search for answers that, of course,
Are found within a Bible source.

'Twas Nehemiah who was called,
By God who told him, "Build a wall"
A wall was built—A nation saved
The people then gave God the praise.

Heaven's jaspered walls of gold,
For believers to behold,
Also has the pearly gate.
This—the true believer's fate.

Because a country cannot be
A country with its sovereignty,
Without some common sense that calls
To be protected by some walls.

Walls symbolize the strength it takes
To protect a Nation State.
And people still can immigrate,
If they come through proper gates.

"Therefore he said unto Judah, Let us build these cities, and make about
them walls, and towers, gates, and bars, while the land is yet before us;
because we have sought the Lord our God, we have sought him, and he
hath given us rest on every side. So they built and prospered."
(2 Chronicles 14:7 KJV)

WHAT TO DO WITH A GIFT

There are three things that one can do
When a special gift arrives.
What you do is up to you,
With your brand-new surprise.

Suppose you do not want the gift—
decide not to accept—
Then you will never know what's there,
Because it was not kept.

You many say "Wow, I do thank you"
And put the package down,
And never open up the thing.
And joy will not be found.

Or, you could open up the gift
Receiving such a thrill
And your life—it will enrich—
Your soul could be fulfilled

There is a present we all have—
A present from above—
And if we chose to take this gift,
We'll find it filled with love.

For god so loved his human race,
He took away our strife
By sending down his only son,
Who gave eternal life.

Do what you choose with Heaven's gift
Don't accept—or do!
Hide it away or use it well—
The decision's up to you.

"For by grace are ye saved through faith; and that not of yourselves: it is the gift of God." (Ephesians 2:8 KJV)

CONSIDER LIFE

Consider life with all its joys, its pain, and sadness too.
Consider all that causes this, no matter what you do.

Some would say that every day is planned out just for you.
Others say your fate's your own as you see your life through.

I believe you make your life (an empty slate to fill),
What you want it to become because you have free will.

So, if you should let go of good and evil takes control,
Then your lives will empty be. The pain will take its toll.

If you believe that you'll succeed and look for good results,
Then you'll be fine—you'll do just great, regardless of your faults.

All people must choose a path and do what they must do;
Whether you choose good or bad, your life is up to you.

"A good man out of the good treasure of the heart bringeth forth good
things: and an evil man out of the evil treasure bringeth forth evil things."
(Matthew 12:35 KJV)

THE ONE WHO WEARS THE CROWN

People say belief in Christ
Is nothing but religion.
In my mind, it's just not true,
No even just a smidgen.

People say they go to church
And just see hypocrites.
They judge God's words by what they see.
No wonder people quit.

But I say if church bothers you.
Because of people there.
And you judge God by their bad acts,
Well that just isn't fair.

If the people in the church
Cause faith to go away—
You haven't put your faith in God
No wonder you won't stay.

Don't put your faith in human folks.
They will let you down.
Your faith must just be focused on
The One who wears the Crown.

"It is better to trust in the Lord than to put confidence in man."
(Psalm 118:8 KJV)

WHO WOULD HAVE THOUGHT?

Who would have thought when we were kids
The entire world would change.
Who would have thought when we matured
Our land would be so strange.

       Who would have thought when we grew up
       That morals would disappear,
       That youth would not listen to truth
       —Just hear what they want to hear.

Who would have thought when we matured
That honesty would be lost
And no one knew what now was true
Or realize the horrible cost.

       Who would have thought when we were gray
       That hate and sin would reign
       And thinking that we could disagree
       Would now be though insane.

Who would have thought when we got old
That some folks could not see
That the ancestors fought and died for us
So we could all live free.

I now think that it's time to change.
It's time to take a stand.
It's time to take a knee perhaps
And ask our God to heal our land.

"But as the days of Noah were, so shall also the coming of the Son of man be." (Matthew 24:37 KJV)

IV

LOVE
AND GROWING OLDER

THE REASON FOR LOVE (IN HAIKU)

I look in her eyes
And see the reason for love.
Beauty shines in her.

She sees me looking
And a gentle smile begins.
It's felt in my soul.

I reach out to her
And our hands feel gentle touch.
Sparks begin to fly.

Two become entwined,
As our bodies become one,
Leaving Earth behind.

We then become still
We realize this is a gift
Not felt by others.

It takes a moment
As we gently share a breath.
Two have become one.

I look in her eyes—And see the reason for love.—
And I thank my God.

"Likewise, ye husbands, dwell with them according to knowledge, giving honor unto the wife, as unto the weaker vessel, and as being heirs together of the grace of life; that your prayers be not hindered." (1 Peter 3:7 KJV)

LOVE NEEDS WORK

They say loves makes the world go 'round
And that sounds good, but I have found,
That love can take one just so far
The rest needs work—a work that's hard.

Nature is (of humankind)
To live on love, but you will find
A love like this could soon grow old,
And if it does, the heart grows cold.

Yes, you must work. Give it your best.
Don't live a life like all the rest.
Create a love that's more than true
And show it by the work you do.

"Nevertheless let every one of you in particular so love his wife even as himself; and the wife see that she reverence her husband."
(Ephesians 5:33KJV)

MY LOVE

The love I have grows more and more.
I must have known my love before.
This truest love—I know for sure,
For she's the one that I adore.

There aren't too many people here,
That wants to hold a soul so near.
To show her, oh, how much I care.
I'm glad I have a love so dear.

"Husbands, love your wives, even as Christ also loved the church, and
gave himself for it." (Ephesians 5:25 KJV)

MAJESTY II

There is no better view for me to see
Then that of Rocky Mountains Majesty.
When setting sun changes the skies from blue
And pinks and then a royal purple hue.

To live within the Mount's security,
Which shares all its abundant life with me,
Is, at least to me, the best of all;
There is no better place I can recall.

I think I'll want my gravestone on this Mount,
When I have reached that time of final rest,
So that my soul can see the setting sun,
When all my work in this world's finally done.

"I will lift up mine eyes unto the hills, from whence cometh my help."
(Psalm 121:1 KJV)

THE EYES ARE JUST THE WINDOWS

The famous quote I love is said like this:
"The eyes are just the windows to the soul."
I've had the chance to see so many eyes—
But when I looked at Hers, my life was whole.

No one knows who really said it first.
I wonder who it was. Who could it be?
Maybe it was told in ancient text,
Or maybe it was Emily Brontë[1]

Something similar was used by Milton,
But others say it's Emerson's reprise.
Cicero just said it was the ears,
But most claim it has always been the eyes.

It doesn't matter who had said it first.
I look into those pools and see my prize.
I understand the gift that I was given,
Because her soul is witnessed in Her eyes.

"The light of the body is the eye: if therefore thine eye be single, thy
whole body shall be full of light." (Matthew 6:22 KJV)

---

1. Author of *Wuthering Heights*, who wrote therein, "Whatever our souls
are made of, his and mine are the same." (81)

COSMIC LOVE

What wonders, I share, that my eyes have seen.
What marvels I've heard in the places I've been.
What beauty my hands, in this life, have touched
The universe filled me with so much.

And the years have crossed my face with lines.
My days have shown me many signs—
Of the hours of love and pain, my friend.
That passes by—toward some end.

The miles I've traveled, both high and low:
The yards, that slowly pained me so—
The feet, that tripped me, if I went too fast—
The inches from danger that allowed me to last.

It's all some plan on a cosmic scale,
That shows me stars, some bright some pale-
And gives me a world to question and love.
I know it comes—from God above.

We all must live upon this Earth—
Beginning with our blinding birth,
And ending in some darkened night
Where we will travel toward the light.

"Through faith we understand that the worlds were framed by the word of God, so that things which are seen were not made of things which do appear." (Hebrews 11:3 KJV)

THE EASTER TRUTH (ULTIMATE LOVE)

What did you do this morning from—9 'til the hour of 6?
What was important during that time? I'll bet—not a crucifix.
But I know one who spent that time hanging on a cross.
He did it for you and He did it for me and He did it to save the lost.

His hands and his feet were nailed to a tree until about the ninth
hour
He chose to stay and die for us all even though He had all power.
When He said—that "It is finished." He finally bowed His head.
Joseph took Him to the burial site because our Savior was dead.

To bury our Lord and Savior, The Christ, Joseph with Nicodemus
Bought 75 pounds of linens and spice to prepare the body of Jesus.
This, too, was an answer to prophecy found in the Holy Word.
David wrote in Psalm 16 so God's message was heard:

"You will not leave my spirit entombed; the Holy one will not decay."
The plan that has been told to you is—He will rise the third day.
Mary Magdalene went to Christ's tomb along with Salome
Mary the mother of James was there the day after the Sabbath day.

When they got there, the tomb was bare and two of them hurried
away.
But Mary Magdalene saw someone and felt she had to stay.
An angel from on high had come, sent by God in Heaven.
He looked at Mary and said these words, Jesus, The Christ, has risen.

Another man who was standing outside said, "Woman why do you
   weep?"
And when she finally saw who He was, She fell at Jesus' feet.
Now go and tell the other disciples and make sure you tell Peter, too.
That which was written long ago, has finally come true.

It is now abundantly clear to all, Christ did what we all have read
As told in the text of prophecies. He has risen from the dead.
He's risen from the dead, my friends and now we can believe.
All you need do is accept Him as Lord—and live eternally.

There has never been another like Him who died to save us all
Standing beside us and holding us up so none of us would fall.
The Easter truth is the ultimate love—the only one to be found
And because of that Love we all can know, that we are Heaven bound!

"For I delivered unto you first of all that which I also received, how that
Christ died for our sins according to the scriptures; and that he was
buried, and that he rose again the third day according to the scriptures:
and that he was seen of Cephas, then of the twelve: after that, he was seen
of above five hundred brethren at once; of whom the greater part remain
unto this present, but some are fallen asleep." (1 Corinthians 15:3–6 KJV)

SANDS AND PEAKS

I saw the sand upon the beach;
It changed each time the waters came.
Although the grains are different there,
In many ways, it stays the same.

I saw the mighty mountain stand
With peaks that stretched to God above,
And though it's changed by age and wear
It's still the place I crave and love.

I saw my one and only love,
With all her beauty, strength, and will,
She says she's changed like peaks and sand,
But as I gaze, I love her still.

"For which cause we faint not; but though our outward man perish, yet
the inward man is renewed day by day." (2 Corinthians 4:16 KJV)

"LIKE" AND "AS"

"Like" a child and "as" a child
Are very different matters.
Like a child is childishness
And I prefer the latter.

"Like a child" brings images
Of selfishness and greed.
Everything must be their way
When wanting more than needs.

"As a child" brings images
Of little ones with faith.
Who accept all things with love
Are humble—full of grace.

Be as a child, not like a child
Depend upon each other.
Forget the hate surrounding you
And just love one another.

"Verily I say unto you, Whosoever shall not receive the kingdom of God
as a little child, he shall not enter therein." (Mark 10:15 KJV)

TO MY WIFE AS WE GROW OLD TOGETHER

She was born this happy day around the time of Spring.
She was born this blessed day with lots of joy to bring
To an adoring home which had lots of love to share,
And was taught from the beginning just how to live and care.

She grew into a woman and never lost her touch
That showed all other people- how she cared so much.
For others needing love and an ear that would attend—
She listened so intently and soon became a friend.

The day she walked into my life changed my heart forever.
It only took one passing glance to know that I could never
Live another day without her splendor by my side—
And then we'd walk together as a husband and his bride.

The years have passed by steadily, through many many Springs,
And life has never changed her soul as each year gently brings
A genuine renewal of the joy that still belongs
To a couple with a love that's true, and happy, and so strong.

"But from the beginning of the creation God made them male and
female. For this cause shall a man leave his father and mother, and cleave
to his wife; And they twain shall be one flesh: so then they are no more
twain, but one flesh. What therefore God hath joined together, let not
man put asunder." (Mark 10:6–9 KJV)

LIFE'S CLOCK

The time was half-past six o'clock
The little one arose,
And did the things that children do.
He had no earthly woes.

He played all day and got his toys—
Until the time for sleep.
He went to bed and closed his eyes
And started counting sheep.

I think it was about twelve—noon,
When he was young and strong.
He'd reached the age he had to choose
Between what's right and wrong.

He gave up toys and choose to work
(Was what he had to be)
And he did what he needed to,
To start his family.

When it was six and skies grew dim,
And time was ticking by,
He took notice of the change.
He knew how time could fly.

He bought some toys and watched awhile
As his own children played.
And then he tucked them into bed.
As the setting sun would fade.

And when the clock struck twelve midnight,
His head had turned to gray.
He wondered where the time had gone,
And how he'd lost the day.

He put away all earthly toys
And knew that it was best,
If he could just prepare himself,
For his eternal rest.

The clock struck six and then struck twelve,
And then struck six again.
Before he knew it night had come.
And he was at day's end

"When I was a child, I spake as a child, I understood as a child, I thought as a child: but when I became a man, I put away childish things." (1 Corinthians 13:11 KJV)

V

DEATH
AND LIFE AFTER DEATH

THE GREAT STORM (A DEATH HAIKU)

The great storm coming
Is one that we all must face.
We don't have a choice.

> Since the beginning
> Men and women realized
> What comes to us all.

For to be living
Means we are all heading to
The end of our lives.

> It is, however,
> A bit easier to go
> If life has been good.

Living for one's self—
Never caring for others—
Causes fear of death.

> Living for others
> Allows us all happiness
> And a different view—

And Living for Christ
Opens the door to Heaven
Because we believe.

"What doth it profit, my brethren, though a man say he hath faith, and have not works? can faith save him? If a brother or sister be naked, and destitute of daily food, And one of you say unto them, Depart in peace, be ye warmed and filled; notwithstanding ye give them not those things which are needful to the body; what doth it profit?" (James 2:14–16 KJV)

MY MOTHER HAD TO TAKE A TRIP

My mother had to take a trip
To lands I did not know.
I spoke to her before she left
To ask her where she'd go.

She looked at me with smiling eyes
And said please have a seat.
I'll tell you all about this trip
To somewhere pure and sweet.

She started to describe a place
Of which I'd never heard.
A glow appeared upon her face;
I listened to each word.

The first thing that she talked about
Were faces bold and fair.
And then she almost shouted out
"See all the children there?"

And then explaining shiny chairs
Especially this one . . .
She stated that she was quite sure
By whom the work was done.

She seemed to stare while pointing at
A special area,
And claimed the angel sitting there
Was "Constalaria."

"Oh Lord," she said, "Do you see, son?
Look—family coming near.
And I can say without a doubt
There's nothing here to fear."

"Someday, my boy, you'll take this trip
And then you'll understand
The beauty here, in all I see,
As I go to this land.

She lay there breathing quietly
But said she wouldn't take
This trip as long as I was there.
She did it for my sake.

I was not there to say goodbye
As mother breathed her last.
It wasn't meant for me to see,
As my sweet mother passed.

Ask me today and I will say
No . . . I will gladly shout.
The gift my mother gave to me
Of Heaven? There's no doubt.

Someday we all will see loved ones
That we lost years ago,
And all of us will take this trip,
To Lands we do not know.

"After this I looked, and, behold, a door was opened in heaven: and the
first voice which I heard was as it were of a trumpet talking with me;
which said, Come up hither, and I will shew thee things which must be
hereafter." (Revelation 4:1 KJV)

THE LIGHT THROUGH US

God created light to pierce the dark,
And others see His light within our heart;
So, we will try to live out every day
To show our neighbors we observe God's way.

We may become distracted and distressed
But God will always help—when we need rest.
Persecution may affect our life.
But Christ will not forsake us in our strife.

They'll cast us down—we'll feel demoralized.
But what God says, what He has authorized,
Can never take away our faith and love
That shows the light, through us, of Christ above.

"Let your light so shine before men, that they may see your good works, and glorify your Father which is in heaven." (Matthew 5:16 KJV)

FINISH LINE

To run Life's race
And call it mine
I had to see
The finish line.

I started first
By running fast
And I thought that
My pace would last.

As time went by
My pace was slowed
Because my eyes
Veered from the road

I missed some steps,
But I was fine
As I ran toward
The finish line.

The race was long.
I thought of friends:
Some at the start—
Some at the end.

Oh, Lord, my race
Took so much time,
But I kept running
Toward the line.

I knew I'd leave
Some friends behind
The day I reached
The finish line.

And when I cross,
With body sore,
I'll see all those
Who ran before.

To Run Life's race
And call it mine
I know I have
To cross the line.

"For we know that if our earthly house of this tabernacle were dissolved, we have a building of God, a house not made with hands, eternal in the heavens." (2 Corinthians 5:1 KJV)

"Let not your heart be troubled: ye believe in God, believe also in me. In my Father's house are many mansions: if it were not so, I would have told you. I go to prepare a place for you. And if I go and prepare a place for you, I will come again, and receive you unto myself; that where I am, there ye may be also." (John 14:1–3 KJV)

AFTER THIS?

If there is nothing after life and atheists are right,
Then how I live while I am here should be for my delight.
There is no one to answer to as we this life embark?
We should see, as they believe, there's nothing but the dark?

Suppose they're wrong about the end. Suppose we ought to give
An ear to men that are so wise who show us how to live.
Oh, is there really something to a God that's always been;
And should we live this life of ours by listening to him?

The answer I believe—you have already guessed.
God is real, He died for us. Then, makes my answer—YES!

"Hast thou not known? hast thou not heard, that the everlasting God, the
Lord, the Creator of the ends of the earth, fainteth not, neither is weary?
there is no searching of his understanding." (Isaiah 40:28 KJV)

WHAT IS LEFT?

All the people who ever lived
Here upon this earth,

Have had a reason to be here
From the moment of their birth.

When we have finally reached the end,
Our life will be defined,

From the words well-spoken by
The ones we've left behind.

"I thank my God upon every remembrance of you." (Philippians 1:3 KJV)

WE KNOW SCIENCE

We know the science of the clouds—   The wind that blows,
   The storm that grows
Into a hurricane.

We know the science of the mind.   The electric flow That
   lets us know
The workings of the brain.

We know the science of the word—   Which makes us able
   To talk through cable
And even through the air.

We know the science of the earth—   The land that shakes
   Because of quakes
That causes ground to tear.

We know the science of the sea—   The waters flow
   The things that grow
Near land and in the deep.

But we don't know the science of—   Our own death—
    That final breath
And where we spend eternal sleep.

Science will not teach us that.   The words of God
    Is what we take,
And all of that is done in faith.

"And be not conformed to this world: but be ye transformed by the renewing of your mind, that ye may prove what is that good, and acceptable, and perfect, will of God. . . ." (Romans 12:2 KJV)

FEARING GOD

When I was young, I was afraid
Of dark things in the night.
Strange noises pounced upon my ears
And logic took its flight.

> I grew to understand dark things
> Not always in my sight,
> Became some object to respect—
> Then, logic ruled the night.

Fear of God is much the same
For all who won't believe.
It's separation from a God
Who they just can't conceive.

> It is a fear of Judgment Day
> With everlasting strife—
> A fear of facing punishment,
> Without eternal life.

For all of those who accept God
There is a difference.
It is based upon respect
With awe and reverence.

> It's wise discernment—true wisdom
> Of a God who will always be—
> The great Creator of us all
> Giving life eternally.

"Thou shalt fear the LORD thy God, and serve him . . ."
(Deuteronomy 6:13 KJV)

BORN AGAIN?

It was Jesus who told us
"You must be born again."
But the choice is up to us.
We decide the "when."

Some think that there is so much time
And there's no need to hurry.
Others say there is no need—
For us to pause and worry.

Just imagine if you are
One who hesitates—
Because you thought you have the time
and plenty—so you wait.

Then, without the slightest warning,
In the twinkling of an eye,
Something happens unexpected—
And suddenly you die.

At the moment when you pass
Without accepting Christ,
You'll be called before the Lord
And you will pay the price.

But, if you make a conscious choice

To take what Jesus gave,
(accepting Jesus as the Lord)
You'll survive the grave.

You were once born to this world
And one day that will end—
Accept the Christ while you're alive
And you'll be born again.

"There was a man of the Pharisees, named Nicodemus, a ruler of the Jews: The same came to Jesus by night, and said unto him, Rabbi, we know that thou art a teacher come from God: for no man can do these miracles that thou doest, except God be with him. Jesus answered and said unto him, Verily, verily, I say unto thee, Except a man be born again, he cannot see the kingdom of God. Nicodemus saith unto him, How can a man be born when he is old? can he enter the second time into his mother's womb, and be born? Jesus answered, Verily, verily, I say unto thee, Except a man be born of water and of the Spirit, he cannot enter into the kingdom of God. That which is born of the flesh is flesh; and that which is born of the Spirit is spirit. Marvel not that I said unto thee, Ye must be born again. The wind bloweth where it listeth, and thou hearest the sound thereof, but canst not tell whence it cometh, and whither it goeth: so is every one that is born of the Spirit." (John 3:1–8 KJV)

WHAT'S UP THERE? (VILLANELLE)

How often I have wondered what's up there—
The place we go when we finish this earth—
Beyond the clouds and way up in the air.

I think it is a place that's more than fair—
A wondrous spot where we will find new birth,
Which causes me to wonder what's up there.

I think that we will live without a care—
A different way to share what life is worth,
Beyond the clouds and way up in the air.

Maybe it's white robes that we will wear—
Well fitted and well tied with proper girth.
Again, I often wonder what's up there.

Will our voices join with others there—
And will our singing be filled up with mirth—
Beyond the clouds and way up in the air?

We will find out when we are gone from here—
As we are given chances for new birth—
And when we find our travels will us bear
To Heaven, and to meet our God up in the air

What's Up There?

"And I saw a new heaven and a new earth: for the first heaven and the first earth were passed away; and there was no more sea. And I John saw the holy city, new Jerusalem, coming down from God out of heaven, prepared as a bride adorned for her husband. And I heard a great voice out of heaven saying, Behold, the tabernacle of God is with men, and he will dwell with them, and they shall be his people, and God himself shall be with them, and be their God. And God shall wipe away all tears from their eyes; and there shall be no more death, neither sorrow, nor crying, neither shall there be any more pain: for the former things are passed away. And he that sat upon the throne said, Behold, I make all things new. And he said unto me, Write: for these words are true and faithful.

And he said unto me, It is done. I am Alpha and Omega, the beginning and the end. I will give unto him that is athirst of the fountain of the water of life freely. He that overcometh shall inherit all things; and I will be his God, and he shall be my son. But the fearful, and unbelieving, and the abominable, and murderers, and whoremongers, and sorcerers, and idolaters, and all liars, shall have their part in the lake which burneth with fire and brimstone: which is the second death. And there came unto me one of the seven angels which had the seven vials full of the seven last plagues, and talked with me, saying, Come hither, I will shew thee the bride, the Lamb's wife. And he carried me away in the spirit to a great and high mountain, and shewed me that great city, the holy Jerusalem, descending out of heaven from God, having the glory of God: and her light was like unto a stone most precious, even like a jasper stone, clear as crystal; And had a wall great and high, and had twelve gates, and at the gates twelve angels, and names written thereon, which are the names of the twelve tribes of the children of Israel: On the east three gates; on the north three gates; on the south three gates; and on the west three gates. And the wall of the city had twelve foundations, and in them the names of the twelve apostles of the Lamb. And he that talked with me had a golden reed to measure the city, and the gates thereof, and the wall thereof. And the city lieth foursquare, and the length is as large as the breadth: and he measured the city with the reed, twelve thousand furlongs. The length and the breadth and the height of it are equal And he measured the wall thereof, an hundred and forty and four cubits, according to the measure of a man, that is, of the angel. And the building of the wall of it was of jasper: and the city was pure gold, like unto clear glass. And the foundations of the wall of the city were garnished with all manner of precious stones. The first foundation was jasper; the second, sapphire; the third, a chalcedony; the fourth, an emerald; The fifth, sardonyx; the sixth, sardius; the seventh, chrysolite; the eighth, beryl; the ninth, a topaz; the tenth, a chrysoprasus; the eleventh, a jacinth; the twelfth, an amethyst. And the twelve gates were twelve pearls; every several gate was of one pearl: and the street of the city was pure gold, as it were transparent glass. And I saw no temple therein: for the Lord God Almighty and the Lamb are the temple of it. And the city had no need of the sun, neither of the moon, to shine in it: for the glory of God did lighten it, and the Lamb is the light thereof. And the nations of them which are saved shall walk in the light of it: and the kings of the earth do bring their glory and honour into it. And the gates of it shall not be shut at all by day: for there shall be no night there. And they shall bring the glory and honour of the nations into it. (Revelation 21:1–26 KJV)

SEE THOSE CROSSES?

See those crosses on that hill,
The three set side by side.
I know the men that they nailed there;
Those three who hung and died.

The first men who was hanging there,
A robber and a thief,
Was not repentant for his crime,
Tho he caused so much grief.

The second was a highwayman,
And sorry for his sin.
He understood he had done wrong—
His life was at its end.

The one placed in the middle
Between two guilty men
Was numbered with transgressors
And never had He sinned.

The first man spoke to the sinless One
(He knew of Jesus there)
"If you are Christ, save you—and us.
Take us down from here."

The other thief rebuked the first,

"Do you not fear God's Son?"
He knew their death was just, and they'd
Been punished for all they'd done.

He looked at Jesus hanging there,
And said, "Remember me."
I want to be in your Kingdom."
Christ said, with Me—you'll be.

Three men died upon that day.
Each had a destination.
The first rejected Jesus Christ
The second—reached redemption.

But the One who hung between the two
Three days laid in the grave.
He then raised up, alive again
And believers were all saved.

To this day we celebrate
Our resurrected Christ
Because He died and rose again,
We reach eternal life.

"Pilate therefore said unto him, Art thou a king then?" Jesus answered,
"Thou sayest that I am a king. To this end was I born, and for this cause
came I into the world, that I should bear witness unto the truth. Every
one that is of the truth heareth my voice." (John 18:37 KJV)

WHY?

Why is it, since beginning time-
There's nothing but questions in one's mind-
A need to know and to create—
To be the authors of our fate?

Why do we ponder our own birth
And living creatures here on Earth,
And why do we always wonder why
That if we live—we all must die?

What is it that's inside of us,
That makes us cry and makes us fuss,
About the daily things we do,
As we travel this life through?

Will we ever know just why,
This thing called life seems to fly by?
Is there a reason that we live?
Will someone please—the answer give?

Or is there just no answer Here?
I think that is my biggest fear.
What shall we do when we're to die?
We'll wait 'till then—and then ask why?

If we wait until we're dead
I afraid that we will dread
The bad decision we have made.
We've missed our chances to be saved.

Maybe we should make our choice
And shout it out in one loud voice—
Don't wait at all, and do what's just,
To follow Him who died for us.

"For now, we see in a mirror dimly, but then face to face. Now I know in part; then I shall know fully, even as I have been fully known."
(1 Corinthians 13:12 KJV)

POINT MAN

Just say we're on a mission,
And I was the point man.
Suppose we had a choice to make
To reach a safer land.

Again, supposed that I just knew
A way to safely reach
A place that we called our refuge,
But I refused to speak.

I think that I'd be derelict
And not so duty bound,
If I refused to show the way
To reach a safer ground.

This situation is the same
When Christ said "Follow me."
Of course, the choice is up to you
To reach sanctuary.

I'd be at fault if I refused
To help your soul survive,
By telling you the only way
To safe eternal life.

Jesus said He was the way—
The truth—The life was He;
And no one comes to God, He said,
Unless it is through me.

It's up to you, accept this gift,
That's all that I can say.
I can't decide what you would choose,
I simply point the way.

"And he said unto them, Go ye into all the world, and preach the gospel to every creature." (Mark 16:15 KJV)

YOUR HUSBAND IS YOUR MAKER

I wondered what Isaiah meant
When he said your husband's your maker.
Since God refers to the church as his bride,
He's describing our Heaven's Caretaker.

God also said there's no weapon made
That will ever succeed against you.
And this includes every man, woman, child—
True believers, both Christian and Jew.

If I understand God's inspired word—
True believers will all be defended.
No scheme designed to destroy the church
Will achieve the outcome intended.

The outcome intended For the Christian Church,
Who Jesus described as a "Wife,"
Is for all His children to be Heaven bound
And experience eternal life.

"Let us be glad and rejoice, and give honour to him: for the marriage of
the Lamb is come, and his wife hath made herself ready."
(Revelation 19:7 KJV)

WHAT DO I DO?

I still am not sure
'Bout the man on that tree.
I don't understand
Why He'd do this for me?

I know I've done wrong.
I've sinned in my life
But, why would this man
Take on all my strife.

What do I do?
How Do I accept,
While all of my sins
In my heart I have kept?

Please help me to know
What I'm s'posed to do
I'm opened—I'll listen
To get help from you.

"That if thou shalt confess with thy mouth the Lord Jesus, and shalt believe in thine heart that God hath raised him from the dead, thou shalt be saved." (Romans 10:9 KJV)

HEREIN IS LOVE
(OR: WHY IT'S A GOOD FRIDAY)

Define the love you have for God
And what He has for you.
One really can't compare the two
For this is surely true:

That He loved us and gave his son,
A victory to win.
'Twas He that came, died on the cross,
Atoning for our sin.

How do we, then, accept this gift
Given by our Lord?
What amount should we all pay?
What can we all afford?

No one here could pay for that,
So, this is what you do.
Open up your heart and say,
Oh Lord, I accept you.

"For by grace are ye saved through faith; and that not of yourselves: it is
the gift of God: Not of works, lest any man should boast."
(Ephesians 2:8–9 KJV)

"But God commendeth his love toward us, in that, while we were yet
sinners, Christ died for us." (Romans 5:8 KJV)

THE THREE MEN THERE

He stood below the three men there and watched as each grow weak.
He simply did his job that day although his thoughts were bleak.
He'd crucified so many men, some bold and some so meek.
These three seemed much like all the rest until he heard them speak.

He heard one man upon the cross, the center one—the Jew,
As He said "Father forgive them, for they know not what they do."
The first man shouted at the one who's cross was in the center.
"You say you're God—You have the power. Free us from our tormentors."

The nailed one who was to the right rebuked the other hanging there.
"Do you not fear Almighty God? Our sins have put us here."
He spoke toward the middle cross—"I'm an undeserving pilgrim.
Remember me, and please forgive, when you have reached your Kingdom."

"I forgive what you have done, for I have paid the price,
And know today that you will be with me in Paradise."
This Roman soldier who stood watch, saw Mary and one—called John,
And heard a voice from the cross that day, say, "Woman, behold thy Son."

This old Centurion from Rome heard Christ, near his last breath,
"My God, my God, why hast Thou forsaken Me" [in death].
The soldier heard the Lord cry out "I thirst." and being kind
Held up a sponge for Christ to drink—a bit of sour wine.

The last things said were, "It is finished." (The guard could barely
    hear it)
"Father, now, into Thy hands, I commend My spirit."
With that Christ died. The soldier cried and stood on blood-
    stained sod.
Then he was heard to say these words, "This was the Son of God!"

"And when the sixth hour was come, there was darkness over the whole
land until the ninth hour. And at the ninth hour Jesus cried with a loud
voice, saying, Eloi, Eloi, lama sabachthani? which is, being interpreted,
My God, my God, why hast thou forsaken me? And some of them that
stood by, when they heard it, said, Behold, he calleth Elias. And one ran
and filled a sponge full of vinegar, and put it on a reed, and gave him to
drink, saying, Let alone; let us see whether Elias will come to take him
down. And Jesus cried with a loud voice, and gave up the ghost. And
the veil of the temple was rent in twain from the top to the bottom. And
when the centurion, which stood over against him, saw that he so cried
out, and gave up the ghost, he said, Truly this man was the Son of God."
(Mark 15:33–39 KJV)

NOW WHAT?

When I accepted Jesus Christ
Out of Love, not fear,
I knew that I was born again.
So where do I go from here?

Jesus died so I could live
He showed what I was worth.
And now I know it's up to me
To shout it to the Earth.

"For I am not ashamed of the gospel of Christ: for it is the power of God unto salvation to everyone that believeth; to the Jew first, and also to the Greek. For therein is the righteousness of God revealed from faith to faith: as it is written, The just shall live by faith." (Romans 1:16–17 KJV)

WE, LIKE THE MOON, REFLECT

Oh Moon, reflector of the Solar Might,
Teach me to brighten dark and dreadful night.
You, who share the sunlight, now unseen
And pierce the darkness with your gentle beam.

You use the Sun which cannot show its rays
Because Rome's Nox[2] has stolen brightened day
And all that's left of sunset is a thought.
The world is filled with shadows darkness brought.

I also feel that I should shine a light
On sullen darkness—hiding in the night.
Where evil sin abides and takes control—
Creating there a hellish frozen soul.

I know that Jesus is the world's pure light,
Defeating sins that hide like darkest night.
I, like the Moon, would use God's light above
To show a soul His way through peace and love.

"This then is the message which we have heard of him, and declare unto you, that God is light, and in him is no darkness at all." (1 John 1:5 KJV)

"Let your light so shine before men, that they may see your good works, and glorify your Father which is in heaven." (Matthew 5:16 KJV)

---

2. Nox is the Roman goddess of night.

V

I AM A SINNER
(Author's Conclusion)

DO WE FOLLOW THE BIG 10?

I know that I am human and filled with human sin. I have, in one way or another, broken the commandments Of God . . . and I would confess that I have probably broken *all* ten. Romans 3:23 tells us "For all have sinned and fall short of the glory of God." I cannot judge you, for that is up to God. I will, however, tell you what I have done and why I made the decision to follow Christ instead of loving the things of this world more than loving God.

To begin, we must look at the Ten Commandments given by God to Moses on Mt. Sinai.

I   "Thou shalt have no other gods before me."

II   "Thou shalt not make unto thee any graven image, or any likeness of anything that is in heaven above, or that is in the earth beneath, or that is in the water under the earth. Thou shall not bow down to them or serve them, for I the Lord your God and only worthy of worship, visiting the iniquity of the fathers on the children to the third and the fourth generation of those who hate me, but showing steadfast love to thousands of those who love me and keep my commandments."

III   "Thou shalt not take the name of the Lord thy God in vain, for the Lord will not hold him guiltless that taketh his name in vain.

IV   "Remember the Sabbath day, to keep it holy. Six days thou shalt labor, and do all thy work, but the seventh day is the Sabbath of the Lord thy God. In it you shalt not do any work, thou, or thy son, or thy daughter, thy Manservant, nor thy maidservant, nor thy cattle, nor thy stranger that is within your gates. For in six days the Lord made heaven and earth, the sea, and all that in them is, and rested the seventh day. Wherefore, the Lord blessed the Sabbath day and hallowed it."

V "Honor thy father and thy mother, that thy days may be long upon the land that the Lord t God giveth thee."

VI "Thou shalt not kill."

VII "Thou shalt not commit adultery."

VIII "Thou shalt not steal."

IX "Thou shalt not bear false witness against thy neighbor."

X "Thou shalt not covet thy neighbor's house; Thou shalt not covet thy neighbor's wife, or his manservant, or his maidservant, or his ox, nor his ass, nor anything that is thy neighbor's." (Exodus 20:2–17 KJV)

First, we should not be worshiping anything other than God. In Matthew 6:24, Jesus warns against the worship of material things. "No one can serve two masters. Either he will hate the one and love the other, or he will be devoted to the one and despise the other. You cannot serve both God and mammon (Money or riches)." I have often looked to money as a way to solve problems. I actually have to admit, at one time, I loved money and it was the love of that money that is evil. At one time, the money I needed was more important than anything. Commandment number one—broken.

Second, I was bowing down to money and worshiping what it could do for me rather than bowing down to God. I was loving and making money my god instead. Also, at one point in my life, I believed that I was more important than anything or anyone else in this world. In all accounts, I was worshiping myself. I was full of pride and greed. It was more than just loving myself because God's creation was important. I was becoming my own god.—Sin 2 God 0.

Using the Lord's name in vain is the third sin which I have committed. Any use of God's name that dishonors Him or shows a lack of reverence for Him is sinful. It is much more than using His name as a curse word. I would tell others that I was a Christian and then live a different life completely. By doing that, by professing God and then not living a godly life, I was a failure. My life's sins are now three for three. At this point I know I am in trouble when it comes to salvation, because *any* sin leads to an eternity away from God.

There were so many years in my life where Sunday was a day used for play and fun. Although I had been raised in a family that never missed Sunday Church and was the grandson and great grandson of preachers, I stopped honoring the "Lord's Day." I had too much to accomplish and to many friends with whom to enjoy a day of fun to take the time for church or for God. I didn't remember the reasons for worship and I certainly never made God's day holy. I broke this Commandment, too.

As far as honoring my mother and father when I was growing up, I fell short here. To honor someone is to show respect, not only in words but in action as well. To honor a person is to revere and to value that person. I always said loved my mother and my father but my actions, on occasion, showed the opposite. There are times now that I wish I could travel back in time and know what I know today. I would have shown the respect they both deserved.

Commandment number six says "Thou shall not murder." I used to think, hey, maybe I did follow the fifth Commandment! I thought I was good on that one until I found out that Proverbs 23:7 stated, "For as he thinketh in his heart, so is he." To be quite honest, I have failed here because there have been times that I wished someone was dead and gone. Hate ruled my heart and not love. God knew what was in my heart and that was just as bad as if I had acted on that hate. I realized I sinned here, too.

The next commandment deals with, and shows that thinking about it is as equal to doing it. I know committing adultery is a sin. I will not go into details here except to say there have been times when I have failed here. Having relationship with someone's wife even if you don't act on it, is a sin. Desiring such a relationship is just as bad as consecrating that relationship. At this point, I know I am lost. I know that I have fallen short of the glory of God.

When I was a child, I took things that didn't belong to me. It doesn't matter what they were. What matters is that I did it. God's eighth Commandment says "Thou shall not steal." If it isn't yours—it isn't yours. It's that simple. No matter what it is, if you take it and it doesn't belong to you, you have sinned. I admit that I was as guilty as can be.

When I was young, I was actually blamed for something I said I didn't do. Actually, I did do it, but I blamed a friend. He then got into trouble. I know I did it because I was scared, but I also knew that I should not bear false witness. In other words, I was causing someone else harm by lying. Jesus, Himself, had false witnesses testified against Him so they could put Him to death. I, just like them, was sinning.

I remember there were plenty of times that I found myself saying, "It's not fair! That person has something, and I wish I had it." What I was doing was disobeying God's tenth Commandment. I was coveting something that I didn't have. As a matter of fact, I was jealous that another person had something I wanted. This sin originates in my most inner being. In my feelings, my heart, my inner self I was showing the sin of envy and this sin is the cause of many of the other sins.

As I said, I had broken all ten of God's commandments. If I had broken just one, I would still be unacceptable in the sight of God. I knew and had read many times that the wages of sin is death. How was I ever to make it up to God? How was I ever going to see eternal life? The only way was found in the words of the Bible. "The wages of sin is death, but the gift of God is eternal life through Jesus Christ." It was God who loved us so much that He gave His only Son to come to this world, live and teach us how to achieve eternal life, and then to die so that we could live with Him even after we die on this Earth. It was a gift. It cannot be bought, It cannot be stolen, it cannot be earned by working for it. All we need to do is to accept the gift and then try our best to live a life that is based on the teachings of Jesus. We will fail. We will sin. We will never be perfect, but we do have a promise. Just as Moses lifter up the snake in the wilderness, so the Son of Man must be lifter up, that everyone who believes in Him may have eternal life. For God sent Jesus to save the world not to condemn it.

Now it is your decision. No one can do it for you. There is no other was to enter the kingdom of Heaven but by Jesus. It is God's gift. It is up to you whether you accept it or reject it. If you decide to accept this gift all you need do is Ask for it. There is no special way to ask, but I have included a prayer at the end that may be helpful. If you do your life is about to change. I would recommend you seek out other Christians and a Bible based church if you wish to strengthen your gift. Whatever you decide just know there are so many people praying for you and so many people who care about you. It is, however, only The Christ who saves you.

IT IS TIME

Oh, children of this ever-sinful Earth,
Who had free will from the moment of your birth,
I've decided I should have this letter sent
To see if you are willing to repent.

From the days of Abraham—
And time and time again
I have given chances for
Your sinful heart to mend.

You have come to me before
And asked me to forgive
And I have done it out of love
Allowing life to live.

I look down upon this sight
That causes me to weep
Because my words of love for you,
You simply will not keep.
You fight and kill your fellow man
And seek to hurt each other.
You hate your Sister and your brother
And your father and your mother.

You're the world that I created,
But you have turned away.
You rejected all my love.
Your sins will make you pay.

So, children of this ever-sinful Earth,
Who had free will from the moment of your birth,
I've decided I should have this letter sent
To see if you are willing to repent.

_____ Signed: GOD _____

VII

APPENDIX

SINNER'S PRAYER

After all is said and done, you, my friend, have a choice. God gave us all free will and an eternal life with him is a gift. You have heard it before: "For God so loved the world that He gave his only begotten Son that whosoever believes in Him shall not perish, but have eternal life." We have all done wrong. We are all sinners and are only worthy of punishment because God is a just God. It is your decision as to whether you want to follow Christ. Jesus was born and was crucified for *you*. He has paid for the sins and the wrongs you have committed and all you need do is accept that gift. The sinners prayer is not a work written by some man who is above all others. It simply asks God to forgive the things you have done against His laws. It is repentance. It tells God that you know He is God and that His son came to save *all* people. Tell Jesus you know He died, was buried, and rose again to defeat death for us. You need to tell him this. Confess with your mouth and ask Him to come into your heart. I can guarantee you will be born again.

The following is just an example of the sinner's prayer. There are many and they are as individual as
you. I pray you decide to accept Christ.

"Dear God, I know I have sinned, and I ask for your forgiveness. I believe Jesus Christ is Your Son and that He died for my sin and that You raised Him from the dead. I want Him to be my Savior and I want to follow Him as my Lord. Guide me and help me to do Your will. I pray this in the name of Jesus. Amen."

If you prayed this, and meant this, you have been born again. I would now suggest that you read His word, and begin to fellowship with others who also believe. I pray for your new journey.

BIBLIOGRAPHY

Bible.Org. "Man Is Made in the Image of God." https://bible.org/seriespage/2-man-trinity-spirit-soul-body.

Brontë, Emily. *Wuthering Heights*. Penguin Classics, 2002.

Cady, Nick. "The Statistical Probability of Jesus Fulfilling the Messianic Prophecies." Theology for the People, February 18, 2020. https://nickcady.org/2020/02/18/the-statistical-probability-of-jesus-fulfilling-the-messianic-prophecies/.

EarthHow. "What Are the 3 Domains of Life?" https://earthhow.com/3-domains-of-life.

Examples.com. "Water (H2o)—Definition, Structure, Preparation, Uses, Benefits." January 28, 2025. https://www.examples.com/chemistry/water.html.

Mac, Emmalise. "What Are The 3 Parts Of The Biosphere?" Sciencing, March 24, 2022. https://www.sciencing.com/3-parts-biosphere-8312194.

Microsoft Bing. "Three Parts Of The Atom And Quarks." https://www.bing.com/images/search?q=three+parts+of+the+atom+and+quarks&qpvt=three+parts+mof+the+atom+and+quarks&form=IGRE&first=1.

NASA.gov. "Building Blocks."' October 22, 2024. https://science.nasa.gov/universe/overview/building-blocks.

National Human Genome Research Institute (NIH). "Deoxyribonucleic Acid (DNA) Fact Sheet." https://www.genome.gov/about-genomics/fact-sheets/Deoxyribonucleic-Acid-Fact-Sheet.

Panchuk, Karla. "Earth's Layers—Crust, Mantle, and Core." https://geo.libretexts.org/Bookshelves/Geology/Physical_Geology.

Schmidt, Doug. "Daily Devo: Fulfilled." The Wesleyan Church, May 8, 2016. https://www.wesleyan.org/fulfilled-5013.

www.ingramcontent.com/pod-product-compliance
Lightning Source LLC
Chambersburg PA
CBHW071441090426
42737CB00011B/1746